Juv
914.5
Rober
2015

WITHDRAWN

D1542316

If you were me and lived in...
ITALY

A Child's Introduction to Culture Around the World

Carole P. Roman
Illustrated by Kelsea Wierenga

To my dearest friends, the Casellas- we'll get there someday!

Special thanks to Connie Giambrone and Lorenzo from the pizza place for all their help.

Copyright © 2015 Carole P. Roman

All rights reserved.

ISBN: 1519241410

ISBN 13: 978-1519241412

If you were me and lived in Italy (I-ta-lja), your home would be called the Republic of Italy, and it would be found in the southern part of Europe. It is often called lo Stivale (lo Stee-val-e) or "the boot," because it is shaped like one.

In ancient times, Italy was the home of the Roman Empire. For many years, it controlled most of the world. At its peak, Rome's armies and outposts could be found in most of Europe, Western Asia, and Northern Africa. The Roman Empire stretched over almost forty-eight modern day countries.

You might live in the capital, Rome (Ro-m-a). Rome was founded by Emperor (Em-per-er) Romulus (Rom-u-las) in the year 753 BC, making it one of the oldest cities where people have continuously lived in Europe. In the olden days, people who lived there were called Etruscans (E-trus-cans).

Rome is the only city in the world that has another country inside its borders. The Catholic (Cath-o-lic) Church is considered an independent state, and its capital, Vatican (Vat-a-can) City, is located there.

Rome is often called the Eternal City and the Caput Mundi (Ca-put Mun-dee) or the Capital of the World because of its influence on western civilization.

Your parents might have picked the name Leonardo (Lee-on-ar-do), Sergio (Ser-gee-o), or Angelo (An-gel-o) if you are a boy. Concetta (Con-chet-a), Giana (Gee-an-na), or Letitia (La-dee-zia) are popular names if you are a girl.

When you talk to your mommy, you would call her Mama (Ma-ma). When Daddy asks if you would like gelato (ja-la-to), you would reply, "Si, Papá" (See, Pa-pa) or "Yes, Daddy." Can you guess what gelato is?

At the store, Mama would use a euro (ur-roo) to buy latte e pane (la-te ee pan-ee) for your lunch. You would say, "Don't forget the prosciutto e formaggio (pro-shoo-to ee for-mag-jee-o) to go on the pane (pan-ee). What do you think you are having for lunch?

If you said a ham and cheese sandwich, you were correct!

When visitors come, you would love to show them the famous Coliseum (Col-es-see-yum) in the center of Rome. It is an ancient concrete and stone theater that is the largest amphitheatre (am-pe-the-ate-ter) in the world. Three emperors or kings built it during the years 72-80 BC. It sat fifty-thousand to eighty-thousand people and was famous for public events. Gladiators (Gla-dee-ate-tors) or soldiers would fight there. Sometimes the floor would be filled with seawater, and great battles would be reenacted.

On Sunday, you would go to Nonno and Nonna's house for a family feast. They are your grandparents and live in the countryside. You would start the meal with a hot soup called stracciatella (str-ja-tel-a), which is a broth filled with egg drops, noodles, and spinach. Nonna is famous for making veal saltimbocca (salt-em-boc-ca) or "hops in the mouth." It is slices of veal cutlet that are covered with prosciutto (pro-shoo-to) or ham, melted cheese, and sage. Nonna would love to make her special spaghetti alla carbonara (spa-ge-tee al-la car-ba-na-ra) or charcoal burners spaghetti. She would make long tubes of hand-rolled spaghetti, adding a sauce of butter, egg yolks, parmigiano (par-mee-jan-o), and pecorino romano (peck-ca-reen-o ro-man-o) cheeses, pancetta (pan-chet-ta) or bacon, and, finally, black pepper. It was the favorite dish of local coal miners, and that's how it got its name.

Of course, every Saturday and Sunday, Mama and Papa would pack everyone in the car and go to watch football at the Olimpico Stadio (Ol-lim-pic-o Stad-ee-o). Thousands of people would be there cheering, and the next day, you would all argue who was the best player.

On March 8th, you would notice yellow mimosa (mim-os-sa) flowers everywhere. Your sibling and you would pick them and present them to the important women in your lives to celebrate la Festa delle Donna (la-Fes-ta del-le Don-a) or International Women's Day. All the women get into national museums for free on this day to celebrate their contributions to culture.

You would also look forward to August 15th, which is the official start of summer and called ferragosto (fer-ra-gos-to). Everybody closes their stores and businesses and heads to the beaches or mountains to enjoy the pleasant weather.

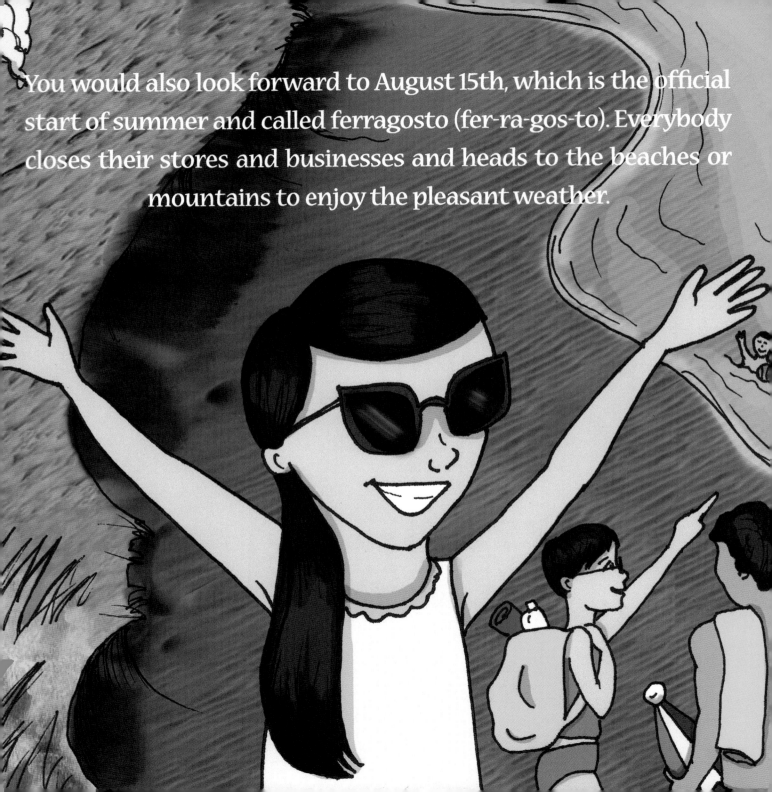

All your friends would have great stories to tell when they go

back to la scula (la scoul-a).

Can you guess what la scula is?

So you see, if you were me,
how life in Italy could really be.

Pronunciation Guide

amphitheatre (am-pe-the-ate-ter)- a large open-aired theater that seats thousands.

Angelo (An-gel-o)- a popular Italian boy's name.

Caput Mundi (Ca-put Mun-dee)- another name for Rome meaning capital of the world because it was important during the Roman Empire.

Catholic (Cath-o-lic)- a religion whose capital city is found in Rome.

Coliseum (Col-es-see-yum)- the name of the famous Roman amphitheatre that is largest in the world.

Concetta (Con-chet-a)- a popular Italian girl's name.

emperors (em-per-ers)- kings.

Etruscans (E-trus-cans)- the name of the original people of Rome.

euro (ur-roo)- money used in Italy.

ferragosto (fer-ra-gos-to)- a holiday that is the kick-off to summer.

football- soccer.

gelato (ja-la-to)- ice cream.

Giana (Gee-an-na)- a popular Italian girl's name.

Gladiators (Gla-de-ate-tors)- Soldiers.

Italy (I-ta-lja)- Italy.

la Festa delle Donne (la Fes-ta del-le Don-a)- International Women's Day.

la scula (la scoul-a)- school.

latte e pane (la-te ee pan-ee)- milk and bread.

Leonardo (Lee-on-ar-do)- a popular Italian boy's name.

Letitia (La-dee-zia)- popular Italian girl's name.

lo Stivale (lo Stee-val-e)- the boot, referring to the shape of Italy.

Mama (Ma-ma)- Mommy.

mimosa (mim-os-sa)- a tree with beautiful yellow flowers.

Nonna (No-na)- Grandma.

Nonno (No-no)- Grandpa.

Olimpico Stadio (Ol-lim-pic-o Stad-ee-o)- the large stadium where sports are played.

pancetta (pan-chet-ta)- bacon.

pane (pan-e)- bread.

Papa (Pa-pa)- Daddy.

parmigiano (par-mee-jan-o)- hard cheese usually grated over food.

pecorino romano (peck-ca-reen-o ro-man-o)- hard cheese usually grated over food.

prosciutto (pro-shoo-to)- ham.

prosciutto e formaggio (pro-shoo-to ee for-mag-jee-o)- ham and cheese.

Rome (Ro-m-a)- the capital of Italy.

Romulus (Rom-u-las)- Emperor of Rome in the year 753 BC.

Sergio (Ser-gee-o)- a popular Italian boy's name.

"Si, Papá" (See, Pa-pa)- "Yes, Papa."

spaghetti alla carbonara (spa-ge-tee al-la car-ba-na-ra)- charcoal spaghetti- a popular dish of coal miners.

stracciatella (str-ja-tel-a)- egg drop soup with noodles and spinach.

Vatican (Vat-a-can) City- independent nation of the Catholic Church that is found within Rome.

veal saltimbocca (salt-em-boc-ca)- veal cutlets with ham and cheese.